HISTORY'S BIGGEST DISASTERS

THE BIGGEST

MILITARY BATTLES

by Connie Colwell Miller

CAPSTONE PRESS
a capstone imprint

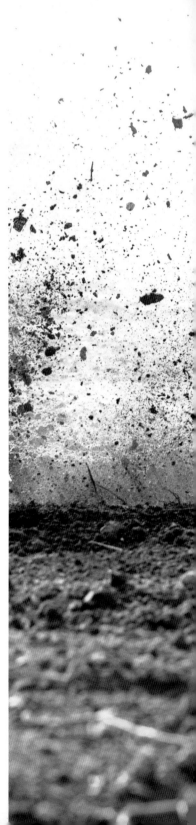

Blazers Books are published by Capstone Press,
1710 Roe Crest Drive, North Mankato, Minnesota 56003
www.mycapstone.com

Library of Congress Cataloging-in-Publication data
Library of Congress Cataloging-in-Publication data is available on the
Library of Congress website.
ISBN 978-1-5157-9989-4 (library binding)
ISBN 978-1-5157-9993-1 (paperback)
ISBN 978-1-5157-9998-6 (eBook PDF)

Editorial Credits
Mandy Robbins, editor; Bobbie Nuytten, designer; Morgan Walters,
media researcher; Tori Abraham, production specialist

Photo Credits
Getty Images: Bettmann, 27, Hulton Archive, 15; Granger, NYC - All
rights reserved, 25; iStockphoto: LifeJourneys, (soldier) right cover;
Newscom: akg-images, 19, akg-images, 21, Ann Ronan Picture Library
Heritage Images, 11, Pictures From History, 9, 23, World History
Archive, 7; Shutterstock: c1a1p1c1o1m1, (dirt) Cover, design element
throughout, Carole Castelli, (soldier) left cover, COLOA Studio,
(smoke) Cover, Crystal-K, (people) design element throughout, Digital
Storm, 28, Everett Historical, 13, 17, fztommy, (dark clouds) Cover,
design element throughout, Jurand, (sandbags) Cover, Michael Mihin,
(soldier) Cover, Mistergoodcat, (explosion) Cover, MoreThanL8ve,
5, Pavel Vakhrushev, 29, Peter Turner Photography, (dunes) Cover,
photocell, (brass plate) design element throughout, Sergey Kamshylin,
(soldier) Cover, Studio 37, (explosion) Cover

Printed and bound in the United States of America.
010753S18

Table of Contents

Deadly Battles

For thousands of years, countries have fought wars. They've changed the course of history. The deadliest military battles have killed millions. Millions more have been hurt.

Battle of
Badger Mouth

August 1211–October 1211

In the early 1200s, Genghis Khan was a powerful leader. His forces attacked the Chinese Jin *Dynasty*. Khan's army was small. But they used clever *tactics*. They defeated the Jin. More than 500,000 Jin soldiers died in battle.

more than 500,000 total Jin deaths

= 10,000 people

dynasty—a series of rulers belonging to the same family or group

tactics—actions taken to achieve a goal

Khan's Mongol forces walked or rode horseback into the Battle of Badger Mouth.

Fact:
About half of the Jin army died during the Battle of Badger Mouth.

Siege of Baghdad

January 29, 1258–February 10, 1258

In 1258 Mongol forces attacked the city of Baghdad. They held the city for 12 days. Around 2 million people were killed or injured. The city of Baghdad was destroyed. Much of its *culture* was lost.

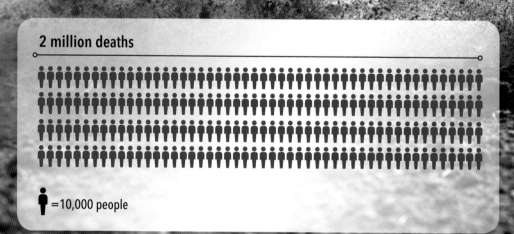

2 million deaths

👤 =10,000 people

culture—a group of people's beliefs, customs, and way of life

Mongol forces surround the city of Baghdad in 1258.

Battle of Gettysburg

July 1, 1863–July 3, 1863

Soldiers fought in the Civil War from 1861 to 1865. The Battle of Gettysburg was the deadliest. It was only three days long. In that short time 46,000 soldiers died. The *Union* officially won this battle. But it lost as many soldiers as the *Confederacy*.

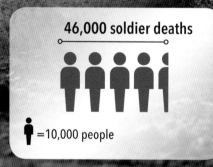

46,000 soldier deaths

 = 10,000 people

Union–the Northern states that fought against the Southern states in the Civil War

Confederacy–the Southern states that fought against the Northern states in the Civil War; also called the Confederate States of America

Union forces advance across a farmer's field in the Battle of Gettysburg.

Fact:
The second day of the Battle of Gettysburg was the deadliest. Around 20,000 soldiers were killed, injured, or captured.

Battle of Gallipoli

February 19, 1915–January 9, 1916

During World War I (1914–1918), the British attacked Gallipoli, Turkey. Turkish gunners hid in the hills. British *troops* marched onto beaches. They were easy targets. After eight months of fighting, more than 500,000 soldiers were killed or injured.

more than 500,000 total soldier deaths

= 10,000 people

troop–a group of soldiers

Turkish soldiers dug trenches into the hills for protection.

Battle of the Somme

July 1, 1916–November 18, 1916

The Battle of the Somme was one of the deadliest of World War I. The *Allies* fought the Germans along the Somme River in France. Almost 70,000 soldiers died on the first day. Fighting continued for three months. More than 1 million people died.

more than 1 million deaths

👤 =10,000 people

Allies–a group of countries that fought the Central Powers in World War I; the Allies included the United States, England, France, Russia, and Italy

The Battle of the Somme featured more heavy guns than any previous battle in history.

German Spring Offensive

March 21, 1918–July 18, 1918

World War I was nearing its end. Germany planned four attacks against the Allies. The attacks were called the Spring Offensive. Around 1.5 million people died. But the Allies held their ground. They won the war.

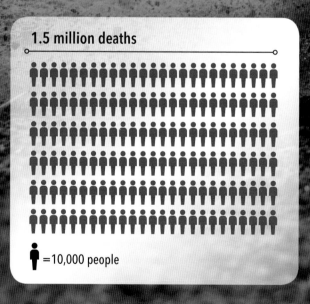

1.5 million deaths

👤 =10,000 people

artillery–large guns, such as cannons or missile launchers, that require several soldiers to load, aim, and fire

British troops defended this French railroad during the Spring Offensive.

Fact:

On the first day of the Spring Offensive, the Germans fired 1 million **artillery** shells at the Allies.

Battle of Moscow

September 1941–January 1942

Early in World War II (1939–1944), the *Nazi* army seemed unstoppable. It attacked the Soviet *capital* city of Moscow in October 1941. Over several months 1 million soldiers died. In the end the Soviet Army beat the Germans.

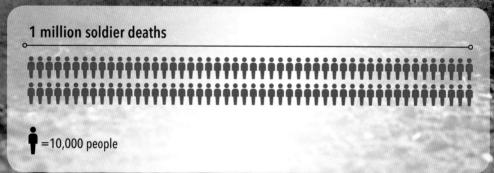

1 million soldier deaths

= 10,000 people

Nazi–a member of a political party led by Adolf Hitler; the Nazis ruled Germany from 1933 to 1945

capital–the city in a country where the government is based

The Soviets shot back at the Nazis with anti-aircraft guns.

Siege of Leningrad

September 1941–January 1944

German and Finnish forces captured the Soviet city of Leningrad in 1941. They held it for 872 days. More than 1.3 million Soviets died. Most were *civilians*. They had starved to death.

more than 1.3 million Soviet deaths

♆ = 10,000 people

civilian—a person who is not in the military

The citizens of Leningrad lived in a war zone for more than two years.

Operation Ichi-Go

April 17, 1944–December 10, 1944

During World War II, the United States and China fought against Japan. U.S. forces were located in southern China. Japanese forces attacked them during Operation Ichi-Go. Japan won the battle. Around 1.3 million people died.

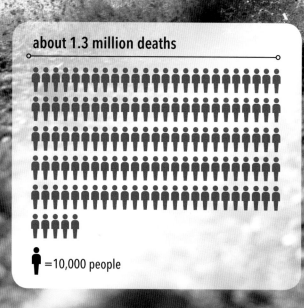

about 1.3 million deaths

= 10,000 people

Chinese forces fight the Japanese from trenches during Operation Ichi-Go.

Fact:

During Operation Ichi-Go, Japan tried to destroy pathways and food that U.S. forces used in China.

Battle of Bloody Ridge

August 18, 1951–September 5, 1951

During the Korean War (1950–1953), South Korea and the United States fought North Korea. Troops faced off over a ridge of hills. Nearly 20,000 troops died in less than three weeks. South Korean and U.S. forces won the battle.

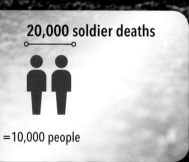

20,000 soldier deaths

= 10,000 people

After 19 days, U.S. troops secured the top of Bloody Ridge.

Tet Offensive

January 30, 1968–September 23, 1968

In 1968 North Vietnam attacked South Vietnam with the Tet Offensive. More than 100,000 people died. South Vietnam and its allies fought off the North Vietnamese. At least 20,000 South Vietnamese and U.S. soldiers died. So did thousands of civilians.

100,000 deaths

🚶🚶🚶🚶🚶🚶🚶🚶🚶🚶

🚶 =10,000 people

The North Vietnamese attacked more than 100 cities and towns during the Tet Offensive.

Future Battles

Military battles have destroyed lives. Cities and entire countries have fallen. Modern weapons cause even more damage. To save lives, leaders must work together for peace.

Glossary

Allies (AL-lyz)—a group of countries that fought the Central Powers in World War I, including the United States, England, and France

artillery (ar-TIL-uh-ree)—large guns, such as cannons or missile launchers, that require several soldiers to load, aim, and fire

capital (KA-puh-tuhl)—a city where the government is based

casualty (KAZH-oo-uhl-tee)—a person killed, wounded, or missing in a battle or in a war

civilian (si-VIL-yuhn)—a person who is not in the military

Confederacy (kuhn-FE-druh-see)—the Southern states that fought against the Northern states in the Civil War

culture (KUHL-chuhr)—a group of people's beliefs, customs, and way of life

dynasty (DYE-nuh-stee)—a series of rulers belonging to the same family or group

Nazi (NOT-see)—a member of a political party led by Adolf Hitler; the Nazis ruled Germany from 1933 to 1945

tactics (TAK-tik)—actions taken to achieve a goal

troop (TROOP)—a group of soldiers

Union (YOON-yuhn)—the Northern states that fought against the Southern states in the Civil War

Read More

Kolpin, Molly. *The Biggest Battles of the Civil War.* The Story of the Civil War. North Mankato, Minn.: Capstone Press, 2015.

Lanser, Amanda. *World War I by the Numbers.* America at War by the Numbers. North Mankato, Minn. Capstone Press, 2016

Nardo, Don. *Bad Days in Battle.* Whoops! A History of Bad Days. Chicago: Heinemann-Raintree, 2017.

Internet Sites

Use FactHound to find Internet sites related to this book.

Visit *www.facthound.com*

Just type in 9781515799894 and go.

Check out projects, games and lots more at
www.capstonekids.com

Index